Becoming
PRESIDENT

By Michael Rajczak

Gareth Stevens
PUBLISHING

Please visit our website, www.garethstevens.com. For a free color catalog of all our high-quality books, call toll free 1-800-542-2595 or fax 1-877-542-2596.

Library of Congress Cataloging-in-Publication Data

Rajczak, Michael.
 Becoming president / Michael Rajczak.
     pages cm. — (Who's your candidate? Choosing government leaders)
 Includes index.
 ISBN 978-1-4824-4039-3 (pbk.)
 ISBN 978-1-4824-4040-9 (6 pack)
 ISBN 978-1-4824-4041-6 (library binding)
 1. Presidents—United States—Juvenile literature. 2. United States—Politics and government—Juvenile literature. I. Title.
 JK517.R346 2016
 324.973—dc23
                                    2015033711

Published in 2016 by
Gareth Stevens Publishing
111 East 14th Street, Suite 349
New York, NY 10003

Copyright © 2016 Gareth Stevens Publishing

Designer: Andrea Davison-Bartolotta
Editor: Kristen Nelson

Photo credits: Cover, p. 1 (Oval Office) Jewel Samad/AFP/Getty Images; cover, p. 1 (girl) Ron Levine/Getty Images; p. 4 David Handschuh/NY Daily News Archive via Getty Images; p. 5 Atomazul/Shutterstock.com; p. 6 Tatiana Kolesnikova/Getty Images; p. 7 (inset) Fotosearch/Getty Images; p. 7 (main) Robert R. McElroy/Getty Images; p. 8 courtesy of the Library of Congress; p. 9 Hank Walker/The LIFE Picture Collection/Getty Images; p. 11 Douglas Graham/Getty Images; pp. 12–13 (buttons) Terry Ashe/The LIFE Images Collection/Getty Images; p. 13 (main) CBS Photo Archive/Getty Images; p. 14 MPI/Getty Images; pp. 15, 16–17 Cynthia Johnson/The LIFE Images Collection/ Getty Images; p. 19 (background) Arina P Habich/Shutterstock.com; p. 19 (map) Mahesh Patil/Shutterstock.com; p. 20 Universal History Archive/UIG/Getty Images; p. 21 George Skadding/The LIFE Picture Collection/Getty Images; p. 22 Jetta Productions/Thinkstock; p. 23 (inset) Kean Collection/Getty Images; p. 23 (main) Visions of America/Getty Images; p. 25 DEA Picture Library/Getty Images; pp. 26–27 Gary John Norman/ Getty Images; p. 27 monkeybusinessimages/iStock/Thinkstock; p. 28 Carlos Chavez/Los Angeles Times via Getty Images; p. 29 Ariel Skelley/Getty Images.

Printed in the United States of America

CPSIA compliance information: Batch #CW16GS: For further information contact Gareth Stevens, New York, New York at 1-800-542-2595.

CONTENTS

Words in the glossary appear in **bold** type the first time they are used in the text.

Enter...the President!

The president is head of the government of the United States of America. He or she is elected by US citizens to serve a 4-year term in office. The president is in charge of the executive branch of the federal government and enforces the laws of our nation.

In your school, the student council president or class president may have similar duties! Student presidents are leaders, and supporting the rules of the school is just part of their job. Usually their term lasts for 1 school year. As a student council or class president, a student leader may help plan activities—and can make a big difference in the school community.

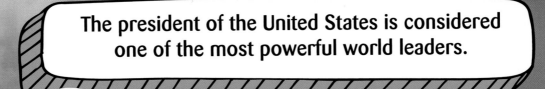

The president of the United States is considered one of the most powerful world leaders.

The Executive Branch

As the head of the executive branch, the president is the commander in chief of the armed forces. The Federal Bureau of Investigation, Central Intelligence Agency, and over 1.4 million members of the armed forces are considered part of the executive branch. Parts of the executive branch monitor parks, collect taxes, and make sure our food and water supply are safe.

Qualities of a Leader

Whether the head of student council or the US government, presidents have certain special qualities that make them good for the job. Confidence, honesty, and responsibility are often important parts of good leaders' character. Voters want to elect people who have proven themselves to be dependable and do what they say they will do. A good leader is also open to new ideas and can make hard decisions when they need to.

Abraham Lincoln is one president who made tough choices for the nation because he thought they were right. He had another quality important for a president to have—the ability to inspire.

Your Turn!

What qualities of a leader do you think are most important? Look around your school and make note of the people who always seem to be chosen by students and teachers to lead groups and activities. They're likely good public speakers, kind to others, and willing to help wherever needed.

President Ronald Reagan won the presidency in 1980 with the inspirational message, "Let's Make America Great Again."

Who Can Become President?

According to the **Constitution** of the United States, only a person who's a natural-born citizen may be president. He or she must have lived in the United States for at least 14 years. A presidential candidate must be at least 35 years old, too. Both men and women may become president.

Presidents have come from a variety of backgrounds. Some were rich like George Washington, but others came from poorer beginnings like Abraham Lincoln. Presidents have been farmers, military leaders, schoolteachers, a university president, and even a geologist. Ronald Reagan had been an actor! Today, most have a background in politics and law.

Abraham Lincoln

John F. Kennedy was the youngest president elected to office. He was 43 when he was elected in 1960.

Your Turn!

There are likely standards you must meet in order to run for class or student council president. You might need to have a certain grade point average or be in one of the higher grades. Some schools have an appointment process for student leadership positions. Be sure to know and follow whatever rules your school has set.

Politics and Primaries

A political party is an organization of people who share similar ideas about how government should be run. The United States has two major political parties—the Democrats and the Republicans. Several people from each party may want to be president. To be an official candidate, a person must have enough party members sign a **petition** of support.

Candidates compete state by state for their party's nomination for president. Some states hold elections called primaries, while other states have meetings called caucuses. These are held in the late winter or spring before the presidential election in November. Whoever wins the primaries and caucuses will become their party's candidate.

Other Political Parties

Political parties other than Democrats and Republicans are called third parties. These are smaller organizations that often focus on just a few special issues. The Green Party's main interest is protecting Earth. Recently, the Reform Party was created based on beliefs that the government needs fixing. As of 2016, no third-party candidate has won the presidency.

The presidential nominee, or chosen candidate, is announced at the Democratic and Republican National Conventions.

Barack Obama

The Campaign

Running a campaign is like selling a candidate to voters. For months—and sometimes more than a year—presidential candidates travel all over the country to tell people what they'll do if elected. Candidates give speeches, do interviews, and hold rallies. They may visit places like nursing homes and factories to meet voters.

An important part of any campaign is advertising. From TV and newspaper ads to mailers and posters, candidates do their best to make their name as recognizable to voters as they can. Today, it's absolutely necessary that candidates have a website and use social media sites such as Facebook and Twitter to reach younger voters.

campaign buttons

BUSH 1988

HUMPHREY
Unity
RESPONSIBLE LEADERSHIP
for PRESIDENT in '68

CARTER 1980

President FORD 76

Michael DUKAKIS FOR President
★1988★

12

TV Debate Time

John F. Kennedy and Richard Nixon had the first televised **debate** in 1960. Since then, the main candidates hold two or three debates that are widely seen on TV. This is a chance for voters to see how the candidates' views may differ. Sometimes debates will have a theme such as foreign policy.

John F. Kennedy

Richard Nixon

RE-ELECT
NIXON
IN '72

Often a campaign uses patriotic colors or symbols, such as a flag, an eagle, or even the Liberty Bell. This is supposed to send the message that the candidate is a person who loves our country.

13

Promises, Promises

Presidential candidates have a message or group of ideas of what they'd like to do as president. It's important for presidential candidates to choose their message carefully. It may be what gets them elected! But campaign promises need to be doable.

When George H. W. Bush rain for president in 1988, he made a promise there would be no new taxes. However, during his term, President Bush and Congress found that new taxes were needed. When he ran for reelection in 1992, voters remembered he broke his promise, and that was one reason why he wasn't reelected.

FOR PRESIDENT

WILLIAM McKINLEY.

WE STAND FOR

The Gold Standard,

Protection and Prosperity,

Just Pension Laws,

And To Redeem All

REPUBLICAN PLEDGES

To The People.

FOR VICE PRESIDENT

THEODORE ROOSEVELT.

poster from William McKinley's second presidential campaign in 1900

Your Turn!

Only make promises you can keep. When running for a student leadership position, find out what you'll be able to do—and what you can't do if you're elected. You could promise free pizza every Friday for lunch, but you probably can't make that happen!

Six words may have kept President Bush from reelection: "Read my lips: no new taxes."

Voting Groups

As the presidential candidates campaign, independent groups use **polling** to see how each candidate is doing. Candidates can use this information to better **target** their campaign. For example, a poll may find that a candidate is popular with men over age 35, but not very popular with women in the same age group. To better reach this group, a candidate may hold an event or put out an ad just for that group!

Who Won?

In 2000, Florida voters had a hard time voting! Paper **ballots** asked voters to punch out holes next to their choices. Some people left the paper hanging on the hole. Others just made a dent in the paper. This caused confusion about the ballot count. The **Supreme Court** stepped in, deciding George W. Bush won the most votes in the state—and therefore won the presidency.

16

Voter turnout can play a big part in an election's outcome. So, when a presidential candidate really inspires a particular group of people, they may have an edge come Election Day.

The 1996 presidential campaign paid a lot of attention to suburban "soccer moms," among whom President Bill Clinton was said to be popular. He won reelection that year.

HISTORICAL MURALS

17

The Electoral College

In order to become president, a candidate needs to win the most electoral votes. Each state is worth a number of electoral votes equal to the total number of senators and congressmen for the state. In most states, the candidate who receives the most individual votes receives all the electoral votes from that state.

Representatives from each state make up the Electoral College. They cast the electoral votes weeks after Election Day. Since there are 538 members of Congress, there are 538 electoral votes. A candidate needs to win at least one more than half this number, or 270, to be elected president.

Future changes?

The Electoral College was put in place at a time when information took weeks to gather. With today's instant communications, many Americans seem to favor allowing the person who wins the **popular vote** to become president. Other people want to keep things as they are.

Electoral Map, 2012 Presidential Election

■ Democrat
□ Republican

Usually, the presidential candidate who wins both the popular vote and the most electoral votes takes office. Four times, the person who won the popular vote didn't win enough electoral votes to be elected.

After the Election

When a person wins the November election, they're known as the president-elect, meaning the next president. This begins a period know as the transition. The person who was president before the election is still president until the middle of January.

The transition from the old president to the new one includes more than just moving out of or into the White House. The president-elect will be busy choosing people for key government positions. He or she may call important leaders of other nations to get to know them. The team of people who helped the president get elected will now help begin to put campaign promises into effect.

Reelection?

Twenty-one presidents have won reelection when they sought it. Four of the 21 had first become president after a president died or chose to leave office by resigning. Grover Cleveland was the only president who won the presidency, lost his reelection, and then won again when he ran a third time.

FOR PRESIDENT
GROVER CLEVELAND,
OF NEW YORK

FOR VICE PRESIDENT
THOS. A. HENDRICKS,
OF INDIANA

LIBERTY   LAW

President Franklin Delano Roosevelt was elected four times! Since then, a constitutional **amendment** has been passed to limit the number of terms a president can serve to two.

The Vice President

Not all presidents are elected for that office. The main duty of the vice president of the United States is to be ready to take on the role of president if the president dies or resigns. Eight vice presidents have become president when the sitting president died.

John Tyler was the first vice president to finish a term for a president who died while in office. Gerald Ford is the only vice president to gain the office because of a president resigning, as Richard Nixon did in 1974. John Adams was the first vice president to win his own presidential term.

Your Turn!

When you're elected as student council or class president, you'll likely have a vice president and other positions under your leadership. While it's important to use your ideas to guide them, asking for their opinions can make your term even better! Working as a team can help you get even more done while in office.

When campaigning for president, candidates or their political parties choose who will be their running mate, or the person who will serve as their vice president. They must keep in mind that a running mate could become president!

Vice President Al Gore

President Bill Clinton

JIMMY CARTER & WALTER MONDALE

LEADERS, FOR A CHANGE.

VOTE DEMOCRATIC NOVEMBER 2ND

Paid for and authorized by 1976 Democratic Presidential Campaign Committee, Inc.

A Very Big Job

The president's main jobs are enforcing the laws of the country and representing the entire nation around the world. He or she often guides the **agenda** of the government. This includes signing bills into law or using the veto power, which stops a bill from becoming law.

It's a big job for just one person. That's why the president chooses a group of advisors known as the cabinet. These advisors are the heads of the departments that make up the executive branch of government, including the budget, foreign policy, and agriculture departments. Their job is to keep the president updated on their department's programs and actions.

Appointees

Cabinet members are appointed by the president and approved for their positions by the Senate. The Senate also approves the president's appointees to the Supreme Court. This helps keep the executive branch from becoming too powerful. There are many checks and balances like this among the executive, **legislative**, and **judicial** branches of the US government.

A position in the cabinet could lead to the presidency! James Monroe served as secretary of state and head of the war department at the same time before he became president in 1817.

25

Your Road to Election!

Are you already a student leader? Being the captain of a sports team or president of a club counts! If you have your eye on a presidential office at your school, it's important to be active in school activities like these.

Make sure you tell people about how you've successfully led groups in the past when running for president.

A student council or class president has many specific duties. These duties are different for each school, so it's important to know what is expected of a president before you decide to run for office. Some are required to be at school board meetings to represent the students. You may need to run activities and lead discussions.

Your Turn!

One of the best ways you can spread the word about your school campaign is by word of mouth. Let your friends and other students know why you want to be class president. Then, encourage them to talk to others. To best get your message across, practice answering questions with clear, short sentences.

Once you become student council or class president, make sure to look back at your campaign promises or message. Fulfilling those promises will likely make others believe your time in office to be a success.

You might have your eye on an even bigger goal—the US presidency! Now is the time to start building your skills for the presidency:

- Learn about politics by being part of a local campaign.

- Sharpen you skills as a public speaker and writer.

- Continue taking leadership positions throughout your time in school.

- Pay attention in history classes to learn how the US government works.

Your Turn!

Even though US citizens can't vote until age 18, that doesn't mean you can't take an interest in the politics around your home and in your state. Do you think a park should be protected or a road better repaired? E-mail your mayor, senator, or congressperson! Practice voicing your beliefs loud and clear.

student council meeting

You can be involved in making your community a better place!

GLOSSARY

agenda: things someone wants to get done or talk about

amendment: a change or addition to a constitution

ballot: a sheet of paper listing candidates' names and used for voting

constitution: the basic laws by which a country or state is governed

debate: an argument or public discussion

judicial: having to do with courts of law and judges

legislative: having to do with making laws

petition: a written request signed by many people

polling: the process of asking questions to find out what most people think of something or someone

popular vote: the choice expressed through the votes cast by eligible voters

Supreme Court: the highest court in the United States

target: the focus of effort

voter turnout: the percentage of those who can vote who actually vote in an election

FOR MORE INFORMATION

BOOKS

Jackson, Carolyn. *The Election Book: The People Pick a President.* New York, NY: Scholastic, 2012.

Lieb, Josh. *I Am a Genius of Unspeakable Evil and I Want to Be Your Class President.* New York, NY: Razorbill, 2009.

WEBSITES

How to Become Class President
wikihow.com/Become-Class-President
Here are 10 steps to help you become class president.

Seven Roles for one President
scholastic.com/teachers/article/seven-roles-one-president
Find out what the president's job includes.

The White House
whitehouse.gov
You can learn more about the White House and even view the president's official schedule.

INDEX